A VOICE FOR THE ANIMALS

BY EVELYN BROOKS

Table of Contents

Introduction

At some time in your life, you've probably seen a lost, **abandoned**, or injured animal limping along the side of a road. Unfortunately, while there are many animal lovers in the world, there are also people who mistreat them. Each day, thousands of pets are abandoned, left on the streets with no one to care for them. Many wander off and get lost.

Suddenly, these poor animals must fend for themselves. They must find food. They must find a warm, dry place to sleep. Often these animals die of hunger and disease. Others are killed on busy highways.

THINK IT OVER!

How do you feel when you see a lost or abandoned animal? Are you angry? Sad? Frustrated? Explain your feelings.

2

What Are the SPCAs?

Throughout the United States, there are many local organizations that work to save the lives of abandoned and mistreated animals. Each organization is known as the Society for the **Prevention** of Cruelty to Animals (SPCA).

The people who work at SPCAs rescue and care for these hurt creatures. At the SPCAs, the animals are cleaned and fed. If the animals are healthy and well behaved, they are offered to people for **adoption**.

Most people think of SPCAs as places to adopt pets.

4

SPCAs across the country take care of huge numbers of animals.

- The Houston, Texas, SPCA serves about 100,000 animals a year.

- The San Francisco, California, SPCA found homes for more than 4,000 dogs and cats last year.

- The ASPCA in New York found homes for about 3,300 animals.

But SPCAs do a lot more than care for stray animals. Here are some of the other important jobs they do:

→ reduce pet overpopulation

→ advise on management of animal shelters

→ promote the investigation of animal cruelty

→ educate people about **humane** treatment of animals

→ provide **veterinary services**

?

Can you use the different percentages to determine how many of each animal were brought in?

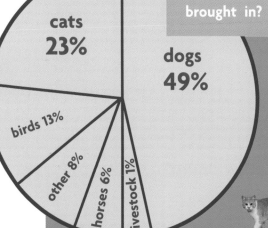

cats 23%

dogs 49%

birds 13%

other 8%

horses 6%

livestock 1%

5

The SPCAs have provided animal care and protection since 1866. Their mission always has been to ease the pain, fear, and suffering of animals. The SPCAs are **nonprofit** organizations. That means they do not take money for helping animals.

Many SPCA workers are volunteers, people who give their time without being paid.

SPCAs help all kinds of animals.

 domestic animals

 farm animals

wild animals

It's a
FACT!

There are
thousands of
SPCAs in the
United States.

Today there are SPCAs throughout the country. There is probably one near where you live. But 160 years ago there were no places for injured and lost animals to go.

7

The Very First SPCA

Animals have been part of people's lives for a very long time. They have provided clothing, food, entertainment, and transportation. They have worked for us and been our friends.

SCIENTIFIC RESEARCH USING ANIMALS

Scientists sometimes use laboratory animals to study diseases and learn how to treat them. Companies sometimes use animals to test new products.

Medical Experiments

The cause of emphysema (em-fih-ZEE-muh), a painful lung disease, is still unknown, and no cure exists. Studies of emphysema in rabbits and horses, however, are helping scientists understand the development of this disease. These studies hold the promise of finding a cure.

Product Experiments

From cosmetics to soap, new products are often tested on animals before they are sold to people. Eyeshadow, for example, is sometimes tested on rabbits to check for eye irritation and other reactions.

THINK IT OVER!

Using animals to study human diseases and to test products is an ongoing debate. How do you feel about this important issue? Have a class debate.

People used to whip their horses to make them work harder.

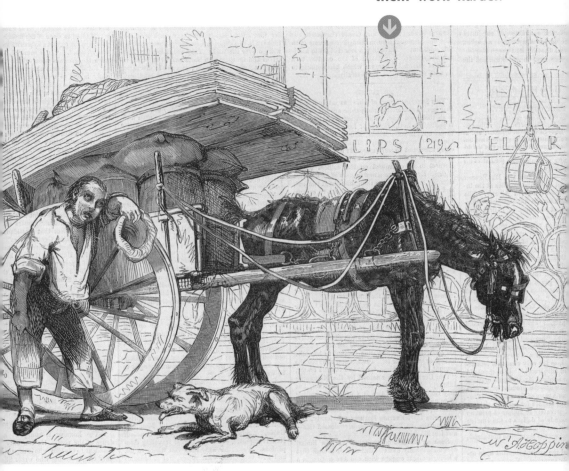

Yet over the centuries, animals have also been abused. Probably no animal has been the victim of more abuse than the horse. Forced to pull heavy carts, wagons, and streetcars, horses were whipped if they didn't move quickly enough. The first SPCA was established to help abused horses and other work animals.

CRUELTY TO ANIMALS—"WHICH ARE THE BRUTES?"—[Sketched by A. R. Waud.]

Richard Martin was an Irishman who worked in the British government. He cared deeply about the suffering of animals. In the early 1800s, he introduced an act, or a formal proposal, to "stop the cruel and improper treatment of **cattle**." It became known as the Martin Act.

This illustration shows many ways in which animals were abused.

In June of 1822, the Martin Act became law. It punished people who mistreated horses, mules, oxen, cows, sheep, and other cattle. People who were caught breaking this law had to pay fines or, in some cases, go to prison. Martin himself roamed through London looking for evidence of cruelty to animals.

ANIMALS HAVE FEELINGS, TOO

Back in the early 1800s, people believed their animals could not feel pain. As a result, people who were usually kind and gentle would whip their animals. Bear fights and setting cats on fire were considered forms of entertainment.

Eventually, medical advances and the invention of the microscope revealed that humans and animals have similar brains and other organs, and that it was possible for animals to feel pain.

Martin's law worked, but it protected only cattle. Other animals were still being mistreated. So the government changed the law in 1833. The new law protected all **domestic animals**, including dogs. Among other things, it made the stoning or beating of animals illegal. It forbade baiting dogs, bulls, bears, and roosters.

Bearbaiting (forcing a bear to fight dogs) was a popular form of entertainment. This fight took place in England in 1820.

12

Queen Victoria was very interested in the movement to prevent cruelty to animals. She helped the RSPCA by giving it money.

Not long after the law was passed, a group of people in London recognized that still more needed to be done to help animals. In 1835, the Royal Society for the Prevention of Cruelty to Animals (RSPCA) was **founded**. Many important people, including the queen of England, supported this society.

13

The SPCA Comes to America

THINK IT OVER!

Henry Bergh once said, "Mankind is served by animals, and in turn they receive no protection."

What did Bergh mean? How do animals serve people? What kind of protection did he have in mind?

A few years after the RSPCA was established in England, the United States passed laws to prevent animal cruelty. People didn't take the laws seriously, however.

In 1863, President Abraham Lincoln assigned a man named Henry Bergh to a diplomatic position in Russia. There, Bergh saw many animals being treated badly by the peasants. The more Bergh saw, the angrier he became. Like Richard Martin in England, Bergh had strong feelings about the way animals should be treated.

14

Henry Bergh cared deeply about the welfare of animals.

Bergh was very concerned about justice for animals. He felt that animals should be given a voice since they couldn't speak for themselves. Bergh decided that he would be that voice.

It's a FACT!

ASPCA vs. SPCA

Bergh's ASPCA in New York City became the model for future SPCAs in the United States. However, only the organization in New York City is called the ASPCA. All others are called SPCAs. Although the ASPCA and the many SPCAs around the country share a common goal, they are not connected officially to one another. Each one is locally funded and operated.

On his return from Russia, Bergh traveled to London, England, where he visited the president of the RSPCA. He learned all that he could about the society. He then returned to New York.

In April of 1866, with help from many businessmen and political leaders, Bergh formed the American Society for the Prevention of Cruelty to Animals (ASPCA), the first SPCA in America. It was the first animal protection agency in the United States. Animals finally had a voice in this country.

This was the original headquarters of the ASPCA in New York City.

17

Bergh encouraged the New York state legislature to pass laws banning cruelty to animals. He also asked it to allow the ASPCA to enforce these laws. The legislature agreed and passed the laws.

The ASPCA went right to work bringing cases of animal mistreatment to court.

One of the first cases involved a man caught beating his horse with a broken spoke from a cart wheel.

Bergh then traveled around the country and spoke to others about the new laws. He inspired people in other cities to form local groups to protect animals.

18

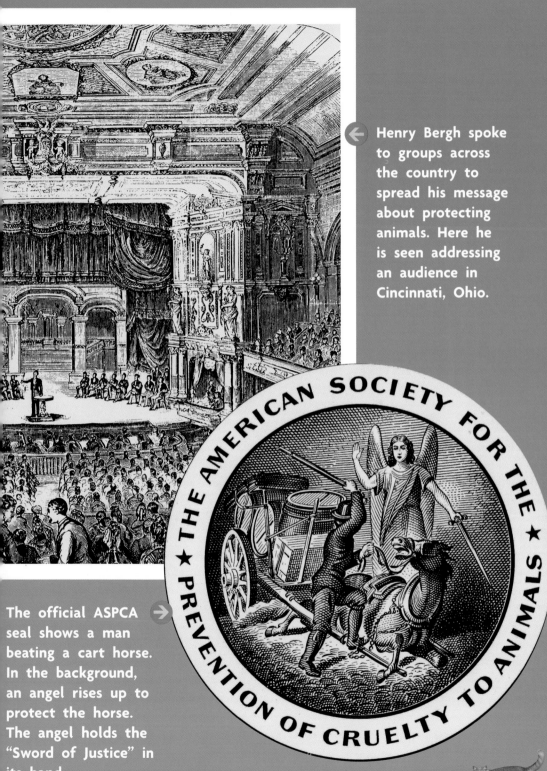

Henry Bergh spoke to groups across the country to spread his message about protecting animals. Here he is seen addressing an audience in Cincinnati, Ohio.

The official ASPCA seal shows a man beating a cart horse. In the background, an angel rises up to protect the horse. The angel holds the "Sword of Justice" in its hand.

★ THE AMERICAN SOCIETY FOR THE ★ PREVENTION OF CRUELTY TO ANIMALS

The ASPCA Goes into Action

Bergh had a special interest in helping carriage horses. Fearlessly, he would go up to people in the street and stop them from whipping horses or overloading carriages.

At first, he gave polite warnings. When he realized that this was not effective, he got the New York City police to enforce the new animal protection laws.

Sick horses were often forced to pull overloaded streetcars. In 1871, Bergh stopped streetcars in downtown New York to protest the overloading of the cars.

The ASPCA operated the first ambulance for horses in the world.

Bergh helped horses in other ways as well. At that time, horses were often injured in their work. Transporting these horses to veterinary clinics was a major problem. Often, injured horses were shot in the streets because it was hard to move them while they were still alive.

In 1867, the ASPCA raised enough money to provide an ambulance to carry sick or injured horses. This was two years before a New York hospital began the first ambulance service for people!

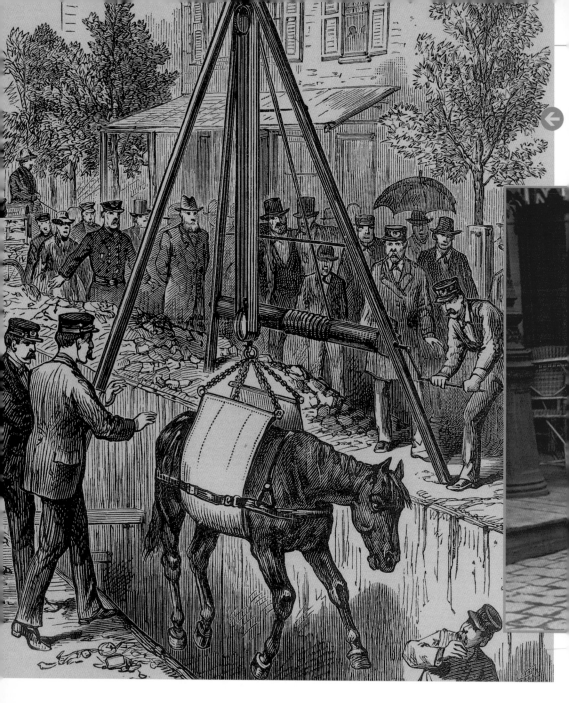

Bergh was also concerned about dogs. Like horses, dogs were often forced to pull heavy carts. Dogs were also made to run on treadmills, or mill wheels that were turned by walking on a continuously moving belt.

Bergh invented the horse sling as a humane
way to lift fallen horses.

Dogs were forced to work until they dropped from
exhaustion.

Even worse were the dogcatchers who
were paid by the city to catch strays.
The dogcatchers would pick up dogs and
puppies and put them into dirty and
overcrowded pounds. Unclaimed dogs
were drowned every afternoon.

Gradually, more and more people became interested in helping animals. By 1873, twenty-five states and territories had agencies similar to the ASPCA.

Henry Bergh died in 1888, but the work of the ASPCA continued on.

SOCIETY FOR THE PREVENTION OF CRUELTY TO CHILDREN

Henry Bergh received criticism for helping animals and not people. But in 1874, a case of child abuse caught his attention. Having nowhere else to go, a social worker approached Bergh about a little girl, Mary Ellen Wilson, who was being abused by the woman she lived with and worked for.

Moved by her story, Bergh took the case to court and won. Mary Ellen was removed from the home and placed with a caring family. Soon after, Bergh founded the Society for the Prevention of Cruelty to Children (SPCC).

This photograph shows a street butcher feeding scraps of meat to stray animals he finds on the street.

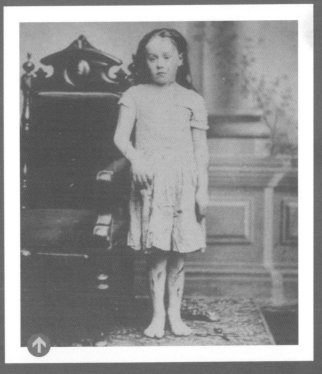

Mary Ellen Wilson was a child in need. Henry Bergh helped her and other children by founding the first child protection agency in America.

25

CHAPTER 5

The ASPCA Grows

By 1894, the ASPCA began to care for stray and unwanted dogs and cats in addition to cattle and work animals. During the early 1900s, the ASPCA continued to expand. It started many services and programs for the care of smaller animals. In 1912, the ASPCA opened the first veterinary clinic in New York City.

This old photo shows students learning about pets.

This veterinarian is examining a horse using the sling invented by Henry Bergh.

In this photo from the 1940s, dog owners wait to attend a dog obedience class.

In 1916, the ASPCA began going to schools to teach students how to care for and respect animals.

In 1944, the society began to hold classes in obedience training for dogs and their owners.

CHAPTER 6

The SPCAs Today

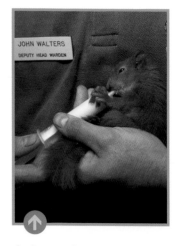

baby red squirrel

Today the ASPCA, SPCAs, and other humane agencies offer shelter, vaccinations, and surgery to **spay** and **neuter** animals. Some local SPCAs even have wildlife centers for animals in the wilderness. The SPCAs also continue to be a voice for animals, tirelessly protecting them from all sorts of cruelty and neglect.

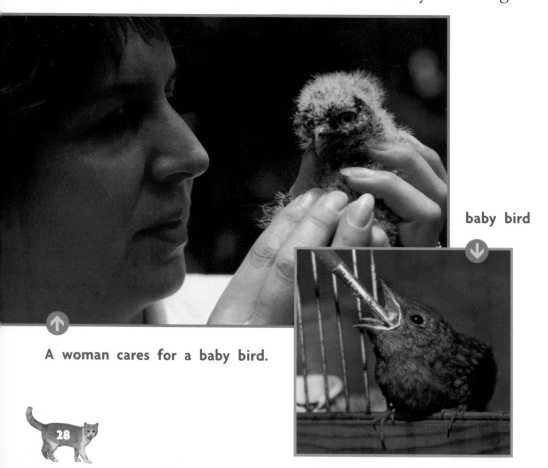

baby bird

A woman cares for a baby bird.

SPCA WILDLIFE CENTERS TO THE RESCUE

Many SPCAs offer medical care to stray and wild animals. It could be an abandoned dog, a deer that's been hit by a car, a pelican that has swallowed a fishing hook, or a hawk with a broken wing. Trained technicians and veterinarians perform operations and give special medicines. After wild animals have been treated, they are returned to their natural habitat as soon as possible.

If you find a stray animal or a wild animal that looks sick or injured, call your local SPCA. Someone will tell you what to do and what not to do until help arrives. NEVER ATTEMPT TO CATCH A STRAY OR WILD ANIMAL BY YOURSELF.

An SPCA volunteer feeds an orphaned skunk.

Milestones in the Formation of the SPCA

1822: The Martin Act, named for Richard Martin, becomes a law in England. It protects cattle from abuse.

1833: The Martin Act is applied to all domestic animals in England.

1835: The RSPCA is founded.

1866: Henry Bergh, a former U.S. diplomat to Russia, forms the ASPCA.

1867: The ASPCA begins running the first horse ambulance.

1875: Henry Bergh invents the horse sling to rescue fallen horses.

1912: The ASPCA opens the first veterinary hospital in New York City.

1916: Humane education program in schools is begun.

1944: Obedience training classes for dog owners are offered by the ASPCA.

| 1800 | 1825 | 1850 | 1875 | 1900 | 1925 | 1950 |

Go To ▶

If you are interested in learning more about the ASPCA, check out the ASPCA Web site: www.aspca.org

This Web site is just for kids who want to learn how to take good care of the animals they love.

30

Glossary

abandoned (uh-BAN-dend) left without any care

adoption (uh-DAHP-shun) the act of choosing an animal or person to become part of a family

cattle (KA-tul) farm or ranch animals that are kept as personal property

domestic animals (duh-MES-tik A-nih-mulz) tame animals, such as horses, cows, dogs, or cats

founded (FOWN-ded) created or established

humane (hyoo-MANE) treating animals or human beings with kindness and sympathy

neuter (NOO-ter) to surgically make male animals unable to reproduce

nonprofit (nahn-PRAH-fit) working without profit or gain

prevention (prih-VEN-shun) the act of not allowing something to happen

spay (SPAY) to surgically make female animals unable to reproduce

veterinary services (VEH-tuh-rih-nair-ee SER-vis-ez) the medical care of animals

Index